Short Wave

By the same author

Poetry Introduction 4 (with Cal Clothier, Anne Cluysenaar, Alistair Elliot, Alan Hollinghurst and Craig Raine)

The Slant Door

November and May

Short Wave

George Szirtes

Secker & Warburg
London

First published in England 1983 by
Martin Secker & Warburg Limited
54 Poland Street, London W1V 3DF

British Library Cataloguing in Publication Data

Szirtes, George
    Short Wave.
    I. Title
    821'.914   PR6069.Z8/

    ISBN 0-436-50996-2

SUBSIDISED BY THE
Arts Council
OF GREAT BRITAIN

Printed in Great Britain by
Redwood Burn Limited
Trowbridge

For Tom and Helen

Acknowledgements

Acknowledgements are due to *Ambit, Argo, Encounter, Grand Piano, The Honest Ulsterman, The Listener, The Literary Review, The London Magazine, New Statesman, Outposts, Poetry Review, The Poetry Book Society New Year Supplement, Quarto, Thames Poetry, The Times Literary Supplement* and *BBC Radio 3* where some of these poems first appeared.

"The Drowned Girl" appeared in Faber's *Poetry Introduction 4*

The Kissing Place sequence was produced by *The Starwheel Press* in 1982 with etchings by Clarissa Upchurch.

Contents

The Kissing Place:

THE SLEEPWALKER

The Sleepwalker

Into this room, which is a pickled darkness
(Pressure sealed, the blinds drawn down)
I blunder, vaguely, stubbing my toes on wood.

This furniture was handed down to us
By my side of the family, and I feel
My way round a low-slung Swedish armchair

That is reassuringly familiar.
The stage is mine now. As I pull
The blinds and open windows the room brightens

And hours fly in. The sofa has come unstuffed,
Light and air play havoc with the props.
My mother leaned on that when she was young

And a young man like a strong wind hung
About her shoulders and her undone lips,
Where that pillow is they sat and laughed.

It all expands, a soap bubble with colours
Delicate and blinding. The street is white,
The sky a cool acidic blue. I float

Within it dizzily, watching the motes
Of dust settle and swirl in a delight
Of movement after the dead hours.

Lilac, Laylock

1. Lilac

Early morning the lilac
quivered, threw out a track
of fragrance to the street,
pervasive, watery-sweet.

The choreography of water,
the drift of scent caught at,
swirling away, blown back,
was the cunning of the lilac.

She bristled sweetness, arched
like a girl. A bullfinch perched
on her crown, immaculate
in his feathers. His weight

bothered the lilac, she bent
a little, her small tent
of pleasure collapsing
inward with the swaying.

2. Laylock

The last place before sleep
in the changing cave;
the children rush to play
rolling on wild grass.

Black cherries fatten us
as we run down the hill.
The flies sleep in the bowl
among the newspapers.

The children dream. They run
towards us bearing faces
that are pinned out like rags
against the lilac branches.

No smell, though garden flowers
are in full bloom
and the queen wasp hovers
about the door.

Abundance

You come to me with that young god
whose hand is slipped in yours, but tired somehow
as if all good were bound to take its toll
and past and future drained what happens now.

In the plenitude of etcetera comes a fullness
satisfying both. Those perfect leaves
can have no weight and are not crushed, your dress,
your open mouth, your eyes made to deceive . . .

The boy who carries grapes and waits to sip
at my half-empty glass already looks
more than half-seas-over. See his lip
unsteady, not, may I say, with reading books.

Hand Dance

They cup or mould or make a shadow
in the full glare of a bedside lamp,
fingers that travel through hair
as on a long journey, or close an eye
preparing for a tiny death or great.
These moved instinctively together
and fell instinctive to such million uses
it seems a shame ever to part them.
How much like each other they've become.
What fine old dances they can twist and turn to,
And think of all the kisses trapped and freed
to catch again, again in the long night
which is longer than their reach or grasp,
which can't be caught by hands and casts no shadow.

Against Dullness

Clouds harbour no cuckoo-land,
preferring fur that wraps up night
like an expected gift.
The chair spins round: a dark unplanned
by schizophrenics comes adrift
and wags a finger out of sight.

I thought you were sitting there,
your hair still dripping from the rain
that lately caught you out.
Tired, you slumped into the chair
and shade and water burned a stain
across the collar of your coat.

Water whispers, makes a dull
provincial sense, and such things may
depress us, being true.
The darkness of the chair was all
that kept the provinces at bay,
half hiding, half displaying you.

Titillations we survive,
and rain too with its gifts of fur
and darkness with its face.
There's little we ourselves can give
but that which loves both rain and fear
and lives in any place.

A Girl Sewing

I do not like you to be quite so still,
only your fingers moving constantly.
I have imagined girls at windows reading,
others sitting staring at a table
lost in the mass of mean forgotten things
that fray or tear almost as soon as finished.
Sometimes the light makes littleness too subtle
so it seems nothing: light so weak that shadows
become indiscernible on a flat surface.

Whole days like this can eat away a life,
leave tiny bones, half powder and half shadow,
freeze the creases of a finished garment
or find perfection in imagined girls.

The Parrotfish

1.
He closed the book and started drifting off.
The night wind hummed and hawed inside his head
then it began to stir about his groin
(but is there any part the wind forgets?)
and so he turned to take her waiting hand.

How gently human hands go their own ways,
laying down a marker here and there.
The stream winds off in thought now they are raised
and stripped and mounted, and her yellow hair
is twisted round between his fingerbones.

Nothing is left but the idea of love,
and real love trailing it so faithfully
that it both seems and is what it pretends,
disappearing, not ungracefully,
where what is longed for hesitates and ends.

2.

The river washes back our skin and seed.
How lovely it is to let go of form
retaining only surface, genitals
that seek the damp and dark of folded petals
and shelter in their hut the rat and worm.

This parrotfish, a bastard shape, a bulk
of beak and rudder tail and greedy eyes
can breathe under her folded sheet of waves.
Indeed we half expect the thing to squawk
or come up with some neatly laundered phrase.

Nature provides fishes with wet graves
from which the spirit flies out like a bird,
flapping and croaking, drying out its feathers.
O parrotfish, a being as absurd
as you is well adapted for all weathers.

Attachments

The radio crackled and crackled and the thin man moved
About his room, spiderwise among the chairs.
His skin was cold, his brow inordinately creased,
A cloth wrung out and left to dry itself.

His name I can't remember — but his room, his brow
Seem of one texture with the noise. He settles down,
Offers me a boiled sweet which I cannot taste.
His living is an absence and a draught.

A Scottish uncle writes to England: Since her death
I do the housework but the furniture retains
Each mark. I'm polishing away her fingerprints
And my whole life is measured in that hand.

An Old Woman Walks Home

If we were machines we would learn movement.
There is a kind of grace appropriate
to function. One could roll along delicately
despite particular conjunctions of fat.

An old slow woman pushing herself home
has tailored her dejection to a style
that is becoming. She understands the force
of gravity more clearly than a child.

That she should move at all is marvellous
but not astonishing. Children burn things
on the wasteground and the ash flies up,
and she would too were she equipped with wings.

It is a question of machinery
and built-in obsolescence. How one fears
for her survival, her immensity,
the enormous effort of becoming tears.

Dialogue for Christmas

This white year arrives and leaves
her gift of boxes crammed with time.
Tomorrow and tomorrow, chime
the little bells to warn off thieves,
but thieves ubiquitous as frost
have entered here and time is lost.

Here they come, the Eastern Kings
laden down with Other Things
fit to please both man and God.
Their boxes open in a flood
of colours bright and cold as snow
that cheer the heart before they go.

What arrives in frost and snow?

The broken branch, the late white night,
a word or echo of delight.

What word is that?
                    I do not know.

SHORT WAVE

Seeing is Believing

"For we walk by faith not sight"

Opening the windows on a receding skyline
   Of regular trees, it seems
That streets, however familiar, are a divine
   Form of architecture,
An autocratic mad professor's lecture
   On the logic of dreams.

A child runs off into the distance
   Diminishing like Alice
With just that stern Victorian insistence
   On etiquette. She disappears
Possibly to drown in her own tears
   Or dine at the Palace.

Horns are mute in forests where a battle
   Hardly rages but dances
To imagined music, and the fallen settle
   On grass and sleep for hours.
The horse of reason champs the brilliant flowers
   And neatly prances.

The Tattooist

1.
He draws the instances and pricks the skin.
He does not have a varied repertoire:
the dragons, banners, naked girls, these are
his offering, his angels on a pin.

One fat customer takes off her bra,
another wants a seascape on his back,
a third one plumps for script with *Ma and Pa*
and coupled hearts below the Union Jack.

The ocean rides along a navvy's arm
and tosses up the mermaids of *The Sun*
whose figures are proportioned like a glass,

who exercise their cumulative charm,
and when he goes about with shirt undone
the tide slips neatly down towards his arse.

2.
Who wears a shirt of water drowns himself.
He pays for luck with loss of appetite:
the lumber of the continental shelf
goes swirling round his stomach day and night.

He flowers into breasts. The mermaids greet
a goddess drifting shoreward on the foam.
The flags are flying all along the street.
The serpents pack their bags and head for home.

May this charm protect him from old age,
from accident, from too much questioning,
from too much sun and too much loneliness.

May the messages relay their message
to bone and heart and may this gaudy Spring
not disappoint him in an Autumn dress.

Goya's Chamber of Horrors

"Ya ya Goya" ("I am Goya") — Andrey Voznesensky

1. The Allegory of the Cloth

His waistcoat runs away down his elegant chest.
The colour pools somewhere just below his heart.
It shakes him with its colds and satins.

The tie that breaks from cavities around his neck
Is a waterfall. His eyes are very wet.
He is indisputably unwell.
Somehow appalled and sentimental all at once
He falls into his own puddle which turns out
Deeper, colder, silkier than paint.

2. The Allegory of the Dummy

He is tossed in a blanket
By cheerful bosomy girls.
He accepts this as his own
Allegory of desire.
When they shoot him he blazes
Like an indulgent omen.

3. The Allegory of Singing

He listens to a woman dying
Who as she dies insists on singing
Though her voice is badly cracking
And nobody else is listening.
She is appalled and sentimental.
He himself finds this appalling.

4. *Yo lo vi — I saw it*

The enemy about my waist
Tears my children in his haste
Lord preserve me live and chaste
    Fear has a sweet and bitter taste.

They hung my arm up on a tree,
My testicles were fed to me
Before I perished. They were men.
    I would do the same to them.

5. *The Allegory of the Enigma*

Construe this if you will. A donkey ride
In hilly country near La Alameda.
All is gentle, all is sonorous
When suddenly a woman falls. The lady
Strikes her head and is concussed.
The gentleman you see there by her side
Is in fact a cleric. What of that?
It need not portend anything at all.
Another lady, dark and beautiful
Expresses consternation, crying out.
But really there is very little cause
For concern. Another gentleman
Admires her eyes and notices her dress
Reveals a shadow somewhat like a bruise.
Perhaps it's simply her time of the moon.
Perhaps this really happened and that lady
Was dressed in such a way as is described.
What is more real? The one who bears the stigma
Of desire? The ass? The memory?
The object of desire to whom is inscribed
Another picture, elsewhere? It is a summery
Day. I am alive and am pleased

To present you with this bright enigma,
The image of a time. Touch it. It is not yet diseased.

6. The Allegory of the Breakfast

He breaks an egg with a sharp tap of the spoon
(Saturn Devouring His Own Children)
Submits a slice of bread to the Inquisition
Of the Fire, wrings the neck of the salt cellar.
Two old macabres make pigs of themselves
On the walls which are horrendous and black.
He rises from the carnage like Colossus.
He cannot hear the agonising creak
Of the chair leg. He cannot hear the shriek
Of the draught that keeps the fire burning.
He stumps about in one of his black moods.
Ya ya Goya, he says, perfectly serious.

John Aubrey's Antique Shop

Certain objects find their way down here —
Grogged in glamour, porcelain faces peer
through flecks of emulsion and faint dust on collars;
shoes go manky, mortuary, scuffed;
the clocks with marbled gingerbead and barley
tell no time but one, the hour of breaking.
And one could find yet bigger, better, richer:
a bellows-organ say with some keys missing
that some doughty Nonconformist household
bright as a button, collars starched resplendent,
trained to Wesley, Lanier and Newton.

As I've forgotten who once said of Andrewes,
his sermons were too playful. I believe it.
"Here's a pretty thing, and here's a pretty thing"
argues a serious lack of seriousness.
In Hell everybody goes dirty all the time.
I once knew a girl as clean as linen.
What would happen to all these did not
such idle fellows as I note them down?

Redcurrants

Acrobatic, the tiny redcurrants
are sprinkled head-first, swollen into scarlet,
and made to dance on crisply gathered points.
Then birds guzzle them or someone picks them
to serve up in a delicate white bowl.
On folding tables in conventional gardens
they glow within an avalanche of cream,
drunk on Lalique, set in a pattern of light.

Sharp, dangerous, the bead memorials
are told without religion, without pain.
Not martyrdom nor a pretence of it
but the fate of jewelry, to go
forth into the world as concentration
without a thing to wear except one colour,
no blood upon the hedge and little taste
and all too small or piqued or plentiful.

A Pheasant

The most beautiful things are not so much
useless as startling: waves that rise in a throat,
the brushed mouths of a pheasant's abdomen,
his blue head lolling on a kitchen table.

Especially in a kitchen the fully feathered
seems like a dangerous gift, shimmering
uneasily under reflected light.
The bird cannot exactly be said to be dead

because his brilliance is undiminished,
and that brilliance was more than half his life.
A dead soldier in full dress uniform
remains a soldier fit for brilliance.

The Bible speaks of ivory and apes.
Of Nineveh and distant Ophir we find
written elsewhere, also the milk-white peacock
drooping moonily in melancholy.

This one here is more the popinjay
caught cold between gags. As Feste says,
"He that is dead needs fear no colours."
The living we are not so sure about.

The Clock Room

1.
Welcome to the Cave of Clocks. The sentries
freeze as you pass through. A ship of brass
prepares to lurch across the table
with its complement of stiffs. A tabernacle
waits like Santa Sophia sheltering
a clutch of domes from Ottoman invaders.

Preferring always what's predictable
you follow with your eyes the jewelled circles
and the Bellman on his dour processional.
Behind a golden door the animators
sing of their monotony; a swineherd
reveals the secrets of the saucepan,
the Princess twirls herself silly,
the bold lover stumbles on to kiss
his Grecian girl again, again, again,
and all the married makers of Geneva
grow melancholy at the sound of bells.

2.
Master Thomas Tompion in his grave
moves on his trochaic destiny
in a world wound round the little finger
of a blind incurious god who pops from boxes.
See his name engraved with flying scrolls,
watch dead courtiers tolling for his death.
Among such stillness such impatience —
the reassurance of a cricket crying.

Rigor mortis has not quite set in —
you do not see the world turn, or your hair
go grey but feel the balance of the stars
disturbed as you brush dandruff from your shoulders.

The seconds draw the minutes; minutes, hours;
hours, days and weeks and months; the weight of years
adjusted on a compensating spring.
Run, run like sand — what else? — you golden hours.
Metal turns to powder when it freezes.

Sea Horse

What has the sea done to them? Her distortions
come sailing at us out of a mirror.
She runs a murky administration
of dead bells and skull-music, dull tirra-lirra.

An urchin turns hedgehog, blows bubbles
to pass the time and keep the living company.
Drowning we eructate through our mouths, sly trebles,
timbreless. There's roaring at the tympanum.

Clouds, horizontals with lump-fish and gurnards,
in turns out, our bones become stars, our eyes
imitate the glasswort, hang like grapes, inward.
Hares are lipped molluscs intent on their disguise.

But among our exoskeletal remains
one creature, but one, may yet come, nosing
shyly between veils of seaweed, gazing down,
its muzzle opening and closing,

not some ten-yard fable raising Proteus
on awesome breakers, but three or four inches, less,
his curlicue of a tail catching at us,
nerves and tendons like old rope; a horse

swimming at us out of the mirror, all wrong.
He will tend to delight whatever stars
are out that night and perhaps bring
with him the drowned and rotten but true cross.

Skeleton Crew

Penelope's suitors chirruped like bats.
Hercules' trained band made bird-like noises.
No one knows what song the sirens sung
or when the air turned music in the lung.

You know what time does to antiquities?
We have museums where there is rejoicing
at a prodigal's return.
The boy who falls to earth but doesn't burn

is an immortal like the piece of wood
miraculously rescued from the Turk.
The flying boys are only made of bone
secreted in some hollow, overgrown.

For forty years these bones have sat and waited.
It's their Hawaii, they her skeleton crew,
coherent bodies whose firm discipline
outlives the aircraft that they travel in.

And now they're found, without names, bleached as Athens.
They waited and their patience is rewarded,
the widows and curators will awake,
the clerks will rectify one small mistake.

But not a shot was fired on Ithaca
though bats were black with panic on the walls,
heads bobbing like a shooting gallery
above another war and frozen sea.

Assassins

My people, by whom I mean those curious sets
Of non-relations in provincial towns,
Sit ripening brightly in the *Weltanschauung*
Of other poets. Here is one who follows
A second-hand pair of shoes into the Courts
Of Social History. Another ransacks
His late unlettered father's bedside drawer
And finds dead ukuleles littered there.
What heraldic yet surreal landscapes!
To lie in the bed of your ancestors
And feel the fit. To hear the neighbourhood
Stirring in its ancient sleep and rhyme
The dead into their regiments of pain.
The poverty of old shoes runs away
With its own eloquence. And yet they write good books.

But I think of an England where the ghosts
Are restless solitaries or assassins.
They cannot speak but run about in sunlight
Demanding restoration of the birch
And death as public as the crime is private.
They have lost time. The Russians on Burns night
Celebrate their history of combustions.
Their people lie in complete unity
In graves as large as Europe and as lonely.

Foresters

Cameron, and his morbid fascination
With gremlins, water-spirits and outlanders
Had them pinned and mounted, a sour nation
Of fearful superstitious peasants
Who drifted into town out of the forests
In search of fresh sea-air and giant crow's-nests,
Talked of vampires and the lycanthrope
And used these comic horrors to scare the pants
Off naughty children and give hope
To balding office wolves for whom
A white neck spelt invariable doom.

But Cameron forgot to give this nation
Credit for their gift of adaptation.
Who faced the baleful gods now faced the sea
And made a certain noise even in the city
And gained success as gatherers of samphire
By infusing native charm with touches of the vampire.

Short Wave

1.
Somewhere in there, in a gap between a taxi
and some indecipherable station
there is a frequency that's unfrequented
like an island, an administration
of ethereal incompetence, the voice of Caliban
deserted but with remnants of quaint speech,
an accent or two that could be out of Shakespeare.

You tune in but the voice is out of reach
and seems merely to flirt with meaning; dry trees
rattling on an unprotected hillside,
hollow tubes wind whistles through. It speaks
at length through a protracted landslide.

Whoever lives here the transmitting tower
is out of date, there is no programme schedule
to list what may be listened to, what hour
the one clear and intelligible accent
will burst like a soprano voice along
the curving sea between the taxi, France
and Germany, all Europe in her song.

2.
This landscape is eternal night — not hell
or purgatory, just a weave of streets
settling like a cobweb late at night
in greys and greens, advances and retreats.

Only drunkards reel home, slam the door
and wander over to the wireless
to turn the dial in hope of finding music,
celestial and perfect more or less.

3.
These reasonable voices going on
and on, unconscionably long
at all hours of the day and night
mean nothing in most places, not to me.
I speak no Dutch or Spanish, tell the truth
I only know my native tongue and French
and that barely sufficient to get by with.

My lips are sour with lager and my head
has no room for a second studio.
Anyway, what do they mean, these voices?
What are they saying? Well, it can be guessed.
Which is why I sit here listening
and turning dials, eavesdropping
on that Balkan baritone
who tells me what the world believes of me.

4.
The planets click like doors or whistle wide.
Their secret messages are understood
by fascinated children in their beds
who're used to lack of sleep and solitude.
Downstairs the broken speech of moving objects
where unrestricted chaos rules the air
and mother is no different from a chair.

We leave the children sleeping and ourselves
lie reading and half listening until
the close-down, when we kiss and frontiers blur
in line with international good will.
There are so many stations on the line,
and other music wells up in the drought
in waves that cancel one another out.

Long Nose Tragedy, Short Nose Comedy

"At the Comédie Française in those days, if you had a long
nose that pointed downwards you did tragedy; and if you had
a short nose that went upwards, you did comedy." (Terry Hands

It's true we are all doomed. Our faces determine
the expressions we find on them. From our childhood
we develop to fulfil their purpose.
We don't like it, true, but then who would?
It is quite possible to preach a sermon
on the limitations of a nose.

Was it a nose that led Jews to their death?
They couldn't cut it off to spite their face
but others are always willing to do it for you.
If it offend thee pluck it out. But what of the space
remaining? It can take away your breath.
You'll never stick it back with Super Glue.

Of course one can make light of the whole thing
while in reality the colours darken
every mood to a deep and steady black
all emanating from the guilty organ.
The sadness of his eminence could bring
tears to the eyes of Cyrano de Bergerac.

It lent him courage too, a kind of glory,
as he himself was never tired of saying.
But Ronsard was a sentimentalist
and bravery is only half the story;
he had heard the hare-lipped woman praying,
Take it away Jesus. I want to be kissed.

Theatre then is a half-baked affair.
Why are you acting so strangely? Who
do you think you are? the old antagonist says.
To which the play replies, And who are you?
Comedy is speeded up despair.
They play straight at the Comédie Française.

Slow Tango for Six Horses

He has of late been swordsman to the Sophy,
Has taken part in Socratic discourses,
Is present holder of the Equine Trophy,
And here he is,
Fresh from Cadiz
With six white horses.

Hold them steady, tight or slack,
Two steps forward and one step back.

Bernarda feels the music in her surging,
Twisting in her harness half in pleasure,
She leads them all because she needs no urging
And prances gladly to the Latin measure.

Two steps forward, one step back.

Arsenic is powder-white and charming,
She enjoys the stallion's protection.
Her manners are both deadly and disarming,
Her kick is deadlier, timed to perfection.

Hold them steady, tight or slack,
Two steps forward and one step back.

Foolscap never looks well but keeps going,
Despite her nerves and constant biting hunger,
Her dance is disciplined and smoothly flowing,
She's building up a reservoir of anger.

Two steps forward, one step back.

Snowdrop loves it all, she is light headed,
She twirls her pretty tail and wears a trilby,
She'll look like candy floss when she is wedded,
She just wants to be happy and she will be.

Two steps forward, one step back.

Blankness is high class but likes the gutter,
Her friends are dirty colts who smell of danger,
How strange they are, some say, but others mutter,
That deep Blankness is the real thing stranger.

Two steps forward.

Catherick is fey, some think she's loony,
A forest spirit only He can summon,
Delicate and mad and flighty-moony,
She claims she is no horse but a real woman.

And so it was just like a dream of horses,
Drifting in a cloud of dicey weather,
Masquerades and elemental forces,
The smell of gunpowder, the crack of leather.
Their trail was smooth and silkier than satin,
The headache a peculiar strain of Latin.

Two steps forward, one step back.

In the Cabbage Grove

The women are walking the cabbage grove
towards a loss they cannot comprehend.
   Quick simple tongues
will click and lips grow wet and spend
their moisture in a ritual of songs
    that pass for love.

They pass beside me, already lost
in shadow and the comprehensive night
   which like a hem
has swept them up, away. What light
perpetuates and mollycoddles them,
    and at what cost?

Admiring their strong legs, their skin
of crusted leather and their death in groves
   of cabbages,
I cannot speak but know their voices prove
the gruffness mine. They are the savages
    I gather in.

THE KISSING PLACE

The Dog Carla

This is what perishes: the soft glut of a chair
in which a white dog perks to her name:
"Come here, Carla. Good dog." "What a coquette
you are, Carla, let us be married at once."
An inverted flower of lace, a crisp head
at the bud, young Philip, heir presumptive
to these darkened rooms addresses Carla.
"What selfish love is this Philip, to imprison
a defenceless dog? You'll pull her tail next!
This is no way for a king to behave."

Philip is the smallest of the dolls.
So lifelike is he that his hope of love
should not go unrealised. He calls to Carla:
"Here dog, here I am, let me stroke you gently."
And Carla skips, Carla fawns! Philip whoops
with laughter to his sister Margareta.
The bells on his petticoat go tonguing
eleisons for conjured Philip,
seriously relaxed now, and exhausted Carla.

Brief Sunlight

What's best of all is sunlight that we feel
only for some ten minutes, even less,
a sudden warmth as if sleeping you had placed
your hand against my cheek in tenderness.

But tenderness is no part of the sun.
Our hands bleach in white heat that carries all
before it like a wave. It's what we feel
that's mortal, tender, paradoxical.

And we are shaken by light in the street,
its angles, jaggedness, its blowsy head
appearing from behind a roof or wall
to lie across our path, invade our bed.

Early Rising

At six o'clock in early March the light
came winding like a sheet about our bed,
binding us into our sleep so tight
we moved in stone between alive and dead.

Our feet were much too far away, our folds
were unremitting, and my hands had lost
all shape and disposition in the cold.
The window frozen with its motes of dust

admitted the high treble of a blackbird
sugaring her benedictions on
a stone garden. Who else could have heard
her sculptured fioratura, neat and clean

as a whistle? Love may last as long
as life perhaps. "Where would we be without
the thought of death to prick us on," she sang,
whose brood of three would not see summer out.

Flemish Rain

In a spindly rain my daughter sits
astride the toilet and makes her own
spindly rain, the tin and copper sound
of water arching out of her,
her belly round, slotted and tight,
swelling out beneath the ribs
of the almost transparent chest
which cradles her neck and the large skull
within its shimmer of flesh. Life there
forms to an aperture, and her mouth
is pinched into a smile of self-consciousness,
hearing both the rains, her own the sweeter.

How am I to give shape to this music
that pours tinkling out of her
but crumbles and powders as it is heard?
A breath of air and it is gone.
I think of Rimbaud's miserable monk
at his grotesque squattings, his bunched
and withered thighs reddening, the stench
a kind of comfort to him, loathsome
in its preternatural sympathy;
and then of one particular boorish Fleming
wetting the thatch beside a house
(I pick her up and shake her)
while a woman flaps her carpet from the window
and the dust shakes out like sunlight.

The Kissing Place

The Claude Glass

A tiny house. The tiny couple move
with the huff and delicacy of birds.
He has the best room and finest view
while she keeps company beside the fire,
brother, sister and all the children
shrunk to a Dutch peep-show, a Claude glass.
The weather holds, a lean boy drives the cows
down to the lake from where the view is striking,
hills and crags bareback on one another
and the house still tinier, still shrinking.

Through the window of a rented farmhouse
I see my wife and children moving dumbly
through a history made picturesque.
In their peep-show all is a pearl stillness,
a singing place for eyes and teeth,
a box to keep absorptions locked away.
The sharp cat is fixed against the floor.
Through the glass you may contemplate the sun's face.

Morning in the Square

The square is empty in the early sunlight.
What is it waiting for? It seems to lack
animation — a delivery van
turns the corner like the shadow of a bird in flight.

It is a kind of delicate mourning —
remaining quiet as if out of respect
for a ritual that has been going on
since the sunset of the previous evening.

Best not to take too much from such retreats
though everything that's peaceful seems to gather
in a broad piazza and the day's arriving
with a shiver down the narrow side streets.

Walls

1.

Is it true the wall is wailing? No,
it is the people. What an articulation
of sound and expressive orders!
They do so ritually as a nation —
it is in their nature to do so.

It is soothing to see great walls, and frightening.
The chicken with its beak against the line
is mesmerised by the sheer enormity
of the idea. Who has the courage to define
an existence so separate, so demanding?

If I see one now I dream it topped with glass;
in the shadow of the wall are people lost
in private acts of faith, good neighbours all
on one side or the other, holding fast
to walls made of ideas and coloured glass.

2.

Wall has its topography
of loose cement and dropping moss,
hillside picturesques and water
seeping through the layers of dirt.

Finding here a dwelling place
you let the world slide under you,
turn Umbrian or Florentine
in a maternal Italy.

Run your hand along the brick
as along a furrowed brow,
a mothering detested damp
like childish mud but colder now.

Porch

Here stood George Herbert not daring
to approach the altar, waiting as do
the young *innamorati* in the last
shelter before their passing through.

Lion, sphinx, pediment
are appropriate. Inside
the cool glissade of hallway
and the noble storeys.

All possibility, an interregnum
between rain and some commitment;
this is the kissing place the god
prepares for us before his passion.

The End of Captain Haddock

Their heads propped on their elbows at the table
are lost in adventures of Tintin and Captain Haddock.
The kitchen grows a beard of fragrance
curling with pomade and vinegar.

Is it Captain Haddock in the pan
cursing softly in his coat of batter?
Whose face is running on the steamed up glass
weeping itself into malformations?

As I Was Going Up the Stair

As I was going up the stair
I met a woman made of air
who seemed a creature half asleep
struggling dreamlike up the steep
demanding incline which would lead
eventually to her bed.
    It seemed to her a dreadful cliff
which she must climb however stiff
and breathless she became, as if
it only mattered to attain
the landing and be free of pain.
    But she was proud to be alone
and pleased to be dependent on
nothing but a wooden rail
between two floors, and this was all
that seemed to her desirable.
It was indeed a kind of game
terminal and dangerous.

Though rooms vary from house to house
most staircases are much the same;
I passed her almost at a run
and when I turned round she was gone.

The Moving Floor

The floor grows away. What distances
it seems to travel! How it rolls in sleep
like water turning in a quiet bay,
calming and disturbing all at once.

From one year old, tottering and grasping
making bull-like rushes at the chair
to five or six when turning dizzily
it spins about us till it crashes upward.

How strange to think of being under it,
supporting a great ship of frozen marble,
all the water traffic of these islands
moving by on cushions of live air.

Bedroom Verse 1

It's true we have our scandals — no one knows
what happened when the lights went out or didn't
or what was said at certain hours of night
beyond the passport office of our clothes,
the secret codeword to the waiting sentry,
the brief descriptions and the formal entry.

Salacious gossip in the daily press
is all the world can speculate upon,
interpreting the drawing of a curtain,
the movement of a shadow or a dress
through an open window, and the breeze
disturbing the composure of the trees.

Common romantic counters of the sort
one finds in certain kinds of poetry
will serve to keep the general public out
who would prefer to read the Hite report.
Can privacy be sordid or obscene?
We'll leave that dark and keep our noses clean.

Bedroom Verse 2

Some people plump for pink or lilac suites,
others go for knobs and canopies,
some do-it-yourself maniacs make their own
in bristling pine, but I think this defeats
the object of both pride and fantasy
and tends to make for boring scenery.

A sweet disorder, no, a downright mess,
as Herrick rightly sang, is more erotic,
though in a bedroom it is not enough
to merely kindle, God knows, wantonness.
Making love is lovely, and so is sleep,
but furniture, like life, can work out cheap.

And here love we lie down night after night
until one day, hey presto, one of us
or both, performs the trick that needs no teaching.
The room for once is really dark. Our tight
embraces were a kind of preparation
for privacy like this, without sensation.

Attic

The spider huddles in its angle like a coat
made small and crushed
and all the dust goes flying down the nearest throat
as if perpetually brushed
by some hopeless, houseproud creature, a disturber
of dreams straight out of Thurber.

I used to think that nightmares entered through the ceiling
and were strangely brought
to my attention like an improper feeling.
They were an alien thought
floating about the town quite randomly
till they took hold of me.

I don't believe that now — I know I can lay claim
to both the nightmares
and the hoarded luggage, and that this uneasy game
is something played upstairs
between the female house, myself and the one ghost
comprised of all that dust.

The Design of Windows

You close it like the good virgin you are
who demands a constancy
appropriate to her stillness. Others would
perhaps lean out (perhaps lean out too far).

By lamplight things appear to strike a posture
that is ludicrous and sad
and vacuous, a bright hole in the fabric,
in every sense an indecent exposure.

Better are the black and unadorned
rectangles of glass, new windows
like negatives, that flaunt their recklessness
in blocks whose shadows leap across the ground.

The Impotence of Chimneys

Silent spouters, barrels, tall comical brothers,
you have reached the age of puberty
and impotence at one and the same time.
The fire in the groin is merely smoke,
the cloud will never rain. How quickly
it disperses and your stumps go gathering
their wits for one pale archaism which
will offend no one. See, even the dead,
how apologetically they fade and blow
above the crematorium, their smoke
invisible, floating about the town
like dandelion seeds. The fat pink Popeye
forearms, the ornate iron hats, are raised
to acknowledge the old Viennese truth
that in between the one fire and the other
we can afford the gentleness of smoke,
secreting pain beneath its decent whiskers
with Lear's menagerie, his nagging cricket.

Join the Company

Allowing a minute's silence for the dead,
a moment's thinking or anticipation,
and noticing a tree
outside the window barely spread
to shield it seems, a world of conversation,
you join the company.

How ancient we all look, the best of friends.
One branch twists in another and the sky
is pale stained glass.
This cold religious afternoon light lends
our faces wisdom, luminosity
which will pass.

So here we stand in one small room, grown wise
but feeling foolish and prepared to laugh
at your return to us.
What would not show in any photograph,
that brief bemused expression in your eyes
of fear and happiness.

Arms outstretched between two periods
the present receives her sentence of lost hours.
Trees disappear
as the light fails. We need the festive gods
to harrow hell and celebrate the power
of the new year.

Turn Again

The pavements lie down narrowing their aisles
against the sunlight which is vanishing.
Their lives are a disappointment to them,
a daily exercise of punishing
self-discipline measured in long miles.

You grab your coat and hat and go outside,
leave doorsteps filthy with anxieties
while treading a fine undulation, cracks
for hopscotch and the promised gold of trees
in autumn, the dull streets of human pride.

Postscript: A Reply to the Angel at Blythburgh

Indeed the Cost of Seriousness
May be death or something less,
A column in the *TLS*
Will do as well.
This long disease my life? Ah yes,
It can be hell.

Hurt "fades to classic pain" you wrote
Yet pain remains, no antidote
Exists however we promote
The Muse of Graves.
The Church's message, and I quote,
Is *Jesus Saves.*

Not death so much then, but the pain.
Religion's task is to explain
What suffering means in the reign
Of good King Good,
Why Blythburgh angels don't complain
Of martyrhood.

Complain? It is a miracle
That angels should survive at all.
True, the woodworm have a ball
Inside her brain.
Her look is faintly comical,
Zonked-out, insane.

Discredited and dull and tame
The churches fear to praise or blame.
They've got themselves a safer game:
The liturgy.
No one goes there all the same
Incredibly.

Residual Christianity
Is ineffective, you'll agree,
The *ut absurdum* to a T.
The Cross demands,
And gets perhaps surprisingly,
Pierced feet and hands.

The Catholics get God *and* Art
(To Puritans they're worlds apart)
The Sistine Chapel for a start,
Georges de la Tour,
While Calvinists, though pure in heart,
Tend to be dour.

But Art comprises *grazie,*
That neat Italianate way
Of making ugly things obey
The rules of dance.
A *contrapposto* sense of sway
Rules out mere chance.

Christ sways on his slender Cross,
St Sebastian, scandalous
In loincloth, sways like Diana Ross,
Supreme, appalled.
Thank God, he cries, I'm not a Grosz
Or Grunewald.

To fabricate or to omit,
To make the hazy definite,
All is fair that Art may fit
Into her scheme.
She'll round a shape to flatter it
Or hear it scream.

She'll hear the scream but make it learn
A civilised and formal turn
Of speech, so that the scream may earn
A living wage.
She makes the devils bake and burn
Inside her cage.

Orcagna, Signorelli — Hell
Is on the whole remarkable
For overcrowding and the smell
Of something rude:
No poise, no sway, no swing, no swell,
No attitude.

Its easiest room is occupied
By those who loved us but have died.
Here Orpheus came to fetch his bride,
A wanderer,
But failed. Is it his face enskied
At Blythburgh?

The expression on that face!
Sometimes in the street I trace
The same ironic commonplace
Look of defeat,
A vagrant, idiotic grace,
Pathetic, sweet.

The common cormorant or shag
Lays eggs inside a paper bag
But does not, like some women, drag
A vast array
Of household junk and filthy rags
Around that way.

That Blythburgh look which reconciles
Apparently contrasting styles,
The daft and Gioconda smiles;
The eyes that stare
Down into the empty aisles
Shield from despair.

Peter, if one verse we write
Shields anyone, however slight
The shelter or how foul the night,
Let's think of her,
And bless the angel's loss of sight
At Blythburgh.